Mentor

*The most important role you were **never** trained for*

By Leon Taylor

Copyright notice

First published 2010 by Soap Box Books
90 Long Acre, Covent Garden, London WC2E 9RZ
www.soapboxbooks.co.uk

ISBN: 978-1-907261-04-6

Printed By Arrowhead Printing Ltd

Forewords

This is the first time, as far as I know, that someone who is a mentor and who has been mentored themselves, has put down their thoughts and guidance on paper. It is a fantastic read and I would recommend it to any parent, coach, business person or athlete who is interested in learning more about how to motivate and communicate effectively in this ever-important role as a mentor. It's a brilliant read – really well done, Leon.

Sir Clive Woodward

Director of Elite Performance, (BOA) British Olympic Association

Mentor

When I found out that Leon was writing a book, I thought what a great idea – he's one of the few people who can pass on experiences as an Olympic medallist and as a great mentor. Leon was my mentor for many crucial years of my career and, without his help, many situations would have been a lot harder for me!

When I was ten, I remember meeting Leon for the first time and asking him for his autograph. He wrote, "To Tom, work hard and success will follow," and ever since then, that has been stuck in my head!

Leon is very laidback as a mentor, which is a great way to be because it puts me at ease. I talk to him often on the phone – we talk over whatever has been happening and it helps me a great deal.

I distinctly remember how much Leon helped when I was learning "the twister" (the world's most difficult dive) because Leon was the person who created it. To get that first-hand experience was something that wasn't available to anyone else in the world.

Forewords

The most memorable moment of working with Leon was seeing him just before I dived in the final of 2010 Commonwealth Games. I had just finished training and I knew I was ready. He had been watching and he knew I was ready, so we said nothing. There was just a nod of approval that simply meant, "Let's do this!" I then went on to win gold.

Tom Daley

World, European and Commonwealth Diving Champion.

Men's 10m Platform.

Mentor

Leon has great eye contact, an engaging enthusiasm, an unswerving sense of honesty, and a Jedi Knight kind of wisdom.

His views on building confidence are riveting.

He has the empathy and good humour that so few attain.

He's a great speaker, a powerful mentor but, with his charm, a "gentlementor" too, whom you know will get the best out of people and make anyone more confident and really up for it.

This leaps to the top of my must-read books on how to boost your adrenalin, confidence and happiness in one go.

If it was a drug, they'd ban it.

Richard Hall

Bestselling Business Author and Professional Mentor

Leon Taylor is my hero. He has cured me of my lifelong fears of heights, water and Speedos. Read this exciting, sensational and wet book if you, too, are looking to "smuggle a budgie".

Justin Lee Collins

Comedian and TV Presenter

Forewords

I worked for ten years (April 1999 to March 2009) as the sport psychologist to the members of the GB diving squad based at Ponds Forge in Sheffield. The only diver who was a constant member of the team for those ten years was Leon. Not only are there enormous physical demands associated with being a 10m platform diver (eg, your body hitting the water at 40mph up to one hundred times a day, six or seven days a week for about 40 weeks a year) but likewise, the psychological demands (eg, fear of injury or failure, and dealing with fatigue) also have massive implications for the athlete.

Throughout those ten years, Leon experienced many "ups and downs", some of which he has shared within this book. The "rollercoaster" that is elite sport places excessive demands on the athlete and to survive the ordeal, the athlete will need a robust set of mental skills, which we often refer to as "Mental Toughness". Confidence, Commitment, Concentration and Control are the key attributes of Mental Toughness and with his usual resolve, Leon developed these in abundance. These qualities along with a willingness to listen and learn quickly and a natural rapport with others undoubtedly underpinned Leon's past successes and will continue to be the foundation for his future endeavours.

Leon's experiences, his positive perceptions and his inquisitive nature will always enable him to find a way forward. These traits - combined with his gregarious personality and excellent communication skills - define an excellent mentor. It is obvious that his clients benefit from his insights, observations and suggestions and that this book will be a very worthwhile addition to your resource base. The comment may be delivered with a nod and wry smile and be a little "tongue in cheek", but it will undoubtedly be worth reflecting upon.

Ian Maynard

Professor of Sport Psychology, Sheffield Hallam University

Mentor

Every now and then a new book comes along which really does add something new to our understanding of performance. This is one of those books, I spent half the time reading and the other half asking myself challenging questions. The focus of this highly readable book is on getting results. Leon Taylor's fascinating insights will help you make better decisions, manage your risks and help increase your chances of success.

This very practical and engaging book positively bubbles with Leon's unerring enthusiasm for mentoring. It is abundantly clear that Leon wants to make a real difference and see his 'Mentees' achieve great things. He is always challenging and whilst he will try to answer their questions, he also questions their answers. Leon's philosophy is to create independence, not dependency and his mentoring is, without question, a transformative experience. He helps people focus on the things that really matter and provides a mixture of stories, questions and insights to help his mentees deal with issues and challenges - but most of all he shows that the solutions are often already within his mentees.

This book is relevant to anyone who wishes to improve their performance in whatever they do. Leon Taylor knows first hand the joys and agonies along the road to winning, he is an inspiring force and a pleasure to work with.

Jeff Grout

Business Speaker, Consultant and fellow Mentor.

Forewords

In this book, Leon invites you to pull up chair, take a seat, and revel in his passion for mentoring others. As someone who has achieved at the highest-possible levels himself, he speaks from a position of authority and experiential knowledge – put simply, his techniques really work when the pressure's on! I hope that Leon's advice has the same impact on you as it has on me.

Dr David Fletcher

PhD CPsychol, Director of Sport Psychology Support Services, Loughborough University

Leon is an inspiration - a real agent of change.
He embodies the skills described in this book and bubbles with infectious enthusiasm.

People change as a result of being in his presence.

This book captures some of the Leon Taylor magic and is a gift to anyone wishing to thrive or help others to fulfil their potential.

Daryll Scott

Author, Trainer of Neuro-Linguistic Programming and High-Performance Coach.

Thanks very much

Writing this book has been real stretch for me in many ways. Those of you who know me or have seen me present on TV will know how animated I am. Unfortunately, waving my arms about while typing doesn't bring the words to life. I even thought I should put the caps lock on and type in capitals if I want to express myself more! I've spent many hours tapping away on my keyboard, struggling at times, but I've made it.

There are several people who deserve a big thank-you for their support and, at times, challenge during this adventure into authorship. Without the mentoring of my dear friend and colleague Daryll Scott, this book would not be in your hand...

For their help, encouragement and valuable feedback, I would also like to thank: Justin Lee Collins, Tom Daley, James Debens, David Fletcher, Jeff Grout, Richard Hall, Lee Hamill, Allie Hill, Ben Houghton, Louisa Huddy, Antony Jewers, Tim Kiy, Ian Maynard, Steve McDermott, Nigel Miller, Mark Mulligan, John Ord, Dom Scott, Adam Sotheran, Nadine Taylor, Peter Waterfield, Andy Webber, Paula West and Sir Clive Woodward.

Contents

ATHENS 2004
ATHENS 20
ATH

Introduction

Hello, my name is Leon and I'm a recovering Olympic diver. The highlight of my career was winning silver medal at the 2004 Athens Olympic Games – British Diving's first Olympic medal for 44 years.

My career spanned more than 20 years and I enjoyed sustained success at the highest level, competing at three Olympic Games and winning medals at all major diving championships.

While I'm immensely proud of this level of success, the thing that fills me with the most pride when I look back is that I was always pushing the boundaries, and in April 1998, I invented "the world's most difficult dive" (backward 2.5 somersaults with 2.5 twists in the piked position). In another sport like, say, gymnastics, I would have been able to name the move after myself, but not in diving unfortunately. The dive description takes longer to say than it does to perform it.

Whenever I look at the back of my Olympic medal, there is a long list of names on it. They're not really there – in reality, it's a load of stuff in Greek, but I see them. It's the names of all the people that were instrumental in getting me onto the Olympic podium.

Mentor

Nothing can prepare you for the bewildering assault on the senses that is the paparazzi at an airport. As the sliding doors part to reveal the arrivals area, the world comes rushing in. There are chaotic movements, shouting, cheering, singing of 'God Save The Queen', questions from all angles, smiling people, camera flashes, waving Union Flags and even more camera flashes. You're suddenly right in the thick of it with no idea what's going on, and unsure of what to do or how to feel. As a friend of mine said at the time, "It's as mad as a box of frogs in here!"

When you are out there, competing at the Olympic Games, you are safely cocooned in an Olympic Village far away from the distractions of the rest of the world; you have no idea what's been going on at home. As we, Team GB, returned home we had not yet re-joined the world; we had an entire plane to ourselves. We were returning with a fantastic medal haul and a few hangovers "to boot".

I had, like many others, enjoyed a few days of non-stop partying, so slept for most of the four-hour flight home from Athens. I awoke as the plane touched down in Heathrow on a gloomy morning at the end of August; well, it seemed gloomy compared to the Greek sunshine I'd been enjoying. The medallists disembarked first, to the cheers of the Heathrow ground staff, and were escorted swiftly through passport control and customs. I remember thinking, "If only it was this easy every time I landed." Before I'd had chance to put my passport away, Peter (my diving partner) and I were hurried forward through the sliding doors and into a sea of madness. That was the moment when I discovered what my medal meant; it already meant the world to me, but in that moment, I realised it was something to be shared; it meant a lot to other people as well.

I had returned to the UK, having won Team GB's first medal of the 2004 Games in the men's 10m syncronised event with my diving partner, Peter

Waterfield. We had put a minority sport on the map and now had the chance to inspire the next generations of sporting stars.

I've always seen this as a kind of welcome responsibility; to share my Olympic medal with as many people as possible, especially young people.

I remember feeling inspired, excited and fascinated, 16 years earlier, when Andy Jameson (the swimmer) sat in the lifeguard chair at my local pool in Cheltenham in front of the whole swimming club and shared his stories of winning a bronze medal at the 1988 Olympic Games. It was one of those experiences that made a massive impact on me, and now it was my chance to do the very same. Interestingly enough, Andy Jameson and I have worked together since as part of the BBC sport commentary team at the Olympic and Commonwealth Games and so I've been able to thank him personally for his inspiration many years ago.

On a typical cold, grey October day in 2004, I was on my way to a Plymouth diving club and taking my opportunity to inspire the next generation of divers. I'd spent many weekends in Plymouth as a youngster competing in both swimming and diving competitions, so the pool held many fond and scary memories. I won my first senior national championship there and I remember so very clearly the leaps of faith and terror in attempting each new dive from the mighty 10m platform. It's one of only seven 10m platforms in the UK and just a 2½-hour drive each way from Cheltenham, so very convenient for my parents and coaches!

I remember taking a call from the coach of the diving club in Plymouth who asked me if I could come down slightly earlier than I'd planned; there was a young diver who was so excited about meeting me. I was his hero, and he was even leaving school early that day because I was coming down. The coach then very excitedly told me that this boy was really good; he'd won this competition and that competition; and he was going to be the next you. I love the enthusiasm of diving coaches; to be honest, it wasn't the first time that I'd heard big statements about young diver's potential from a coach. I, of course, said yes and didn't really think much of it. This was, after all, what I was here to do – to meet youngsters and inspire them.

I remember meeting Tom in the café area at the pool in Plymouth. He looked like your average ten-year-old – a small, brown-haired boy in a tracksuit. I immediately burst into my usual line of questions in order to put him at ease "so how long have you been diving?"; "did you enjoy watching the Olympic Games?" and so on. Yet, within two minutes of meeting him, I'm asking myself: "Are you sure that this kid is ten years old?" Having had many an awkward conversation with nervous youngsters before, this was very different. I was the one replying to open questions and feeling at ease. There was something about this young boy, something very special, something indescribable. The voice in my head kept saying: "Are you sure that this kid is only ten?"

After 30 minutes or so of chat, I had the chance to watch Tom practise some of his dives. So off he went to warm up and I spoke to the coach: "What an amazing young boy!" I said. "Wait until you see him in the pool," he retorted.

Holy moly! I will never forget that moment. My jaw hit the floor – I couldn't believe what I was seeing. This kid is the real deal; the coaches weren't exaggerating about how much potential there was. He had it all going on. What a talent. The most talented young diver I had ever seen anywhere. I was completely blown away.

I thought two things – the first was, "Damn, I wish I was that good when I was ten".

The second was, ***wouldn't it be great if I could get what is in my head into his head, how good could he be then?***

Introduction

Imagine if he could have all my experiences and learning from those 19 years in the sport? He could be so much better than me.

I offered to become Tom's mentor and he accepted! He already had a great diving coach, supportive parents and a fantastic team. I would play a different role. We chatted for a while longer after he'd finished in the pool and it was set – I was to be Tom's mentor.

Like a giddy child, I wanted to tell him everything at once! But because of my many years as an Olympic performer, I know exactly what it's like to be on the receiving end of too much advice. A dive from the 10m takes 1.5 seconds; I've had coaches bombard me with ten pieces of advice to implement into my next dive! Just one or two pieces at a time please.

Being coached and mentored for so many years to such a high standard has provided a great perspective on the many ways in which to mentor others. There is not a one-size-fits-all approach and a good mentor is flexible enough to choose different approaches based on what's going on for the mentee at the time.

I always wanted to do more than tell my Olympic story. Like those of most Olympians, my story has many great metaphors that are useful and timeless, but I wanted to go further. I wanted to make sure that it stays relevant and delivers real value to my audiences whether they are teenagers or corporate execs.

Mentoring is the first area that I fell compelled to explore even further because ***it's my personal opinion that real mentoring is a bit of a forgotten art in our society.***

You are probably wondering what to expect from this book...

Mentor

I have been mentored to achieve at the highest level of performance and have spent much of the time after my competition days being a mentor to others. I have experienced different results and become aware that there is more to it than telling people about your knowledge and experience; there is a need to put it across in a way that works.

I'm sure that you can remember your experience of different school teachers, they had the same training and they were working from the same syllabus but the results were different because of how they did it – some teachers you remember and they said things that have stayed with you, others you have already forgotten. You can apply this observation to anyone; bosses, co-workers, celebrities, comedians, family members; any human communication.

This book is not about the concept of mentoring, or best practice for setting up mentoring programmes, or how to select or approach a mentor. ***It's about being a mentor.***

At the time of writing, I am being mentored to become a Master Practitioner in Neurotic-Linguistic Programming (NLP). As I explore the patterns of NLP more and more deeply, I am finding a lot of the techniques echo my real experiences and provide me with a way of describing what happened when mentoring relationships were very effective.

There is a big difference between knowing what a mentor should be (the ability to talk about it) and having the attitude, behaviour and communication skills to be one (the ability to do it).

In this book, I'm hoping to provide some simple techniques that will help with the "doing" part of mentoring. Within each chapter, I tell an autobiographical story with the intention of making it entertaining, bringing the context to life and clearly demonstrating an approach. I will then go on to be explicit about the relevant take-away technique, which can be used in any important relationship whether you are a mentor, parent, teacher or friend.

This book is my approach to mentoring, I'm not presenting it as fact or suggesting that there is a right/wrong approach. It's not a seven-step model and there is no sequence to the techniques – you use them when you need them.

These are my real experiences, and the techniques that I use, and they work. I have been quite open and frank about my attitude to mentoring – how much you take away is of course up to you – I would suggest as much as you can get away with. Either way, I hope that you can see the relevance and that you enjoy my first book.

What is MENTORING?

Have you ever noticed how children and their grandparents get on so well? Some say it's because they have a shared enemy!

It's easy to observe how differently grandparents behave. Generally, they seem to be more patient. They often have more time; in many cases, they come down to the children's level to talk with them. We can all imagine an image of the archetypal grandparent, sitting forward in the armchair and really engaging with the grandchild. They sometimes affectionately tease the kids, or play along with them in their world. Because they are often not attempting to discipline or control the children they have the flexibility to simply enjoy the connection through playful communication.

For the best results, it is generally agreed that there are a few important factors that add up to a great mentoring connection and experience. It's certainly important that a mentor is extremely supportive. It's important that they have no hidden agenda or vested interest; they need to be non-judgmental, and accept that sometimes the most valuable interactions will go off at a tangent.

A mentor plays a very parental role; but it's not like a parent with their rules, instructions and inflexibilities. A great mentor is more like a grandparent, more tolerant, more patient and less judgmental.

In many contexts, mentoring is very similar to coaching, the difference being as a mentor you've been there, done it and bought the T-shirt; and you share the benefit of your experience.

"Mentoring is a brain to pick, an ear to listen, and a push in the right direction" John Crosby

What is MENTORING?

Mentoring is a pretty intimate relationship; there are so many facets to life and all will have an effect on performance. As a mentor, you're likely to find yourself exploring more personal challenges that, if dealt with well, have a massive positive impact. It's looking at the big picture and talking about causes, not just symptoms. It's about supporting the mentee on their journey.

But support isn't everything; it's only one side of the equation. It's unlikely anyone was ever comforted into high-performance. As a mentor, you are supporting people to encourage them to push their comfort zones, to strive, and grow.

Support is essential, but it's not enough you may also need to gently challenge to evoke determination, curiosity, motivation, obsessive focus and maybe even temporary frustration.

There is a good degree of rapport and positively intended playfulness involved in doing this effectively, and the mentee needs to be up for being pushed a little for their own best interests – whether that is affectionately pointing out where the mentee has made a poor choice and maybe making a joke of it, withholding the answer so that the mentee is required to keep thinking, or a direct challenge that is clearly positive and supportive – "Come on, you can do better than that."

On some occasions, the most effective thing you can do as a mentor is bite your lip and say nothing; resisting the temptation to contribute or give advice and instead, just listen. Ask the occasional question, listen some more and watch as your mentee challenges themself to unravel the problem and come up with alternatives.

When you are being mentored it's usually just one statement, one question, one story, one observation that shifts your thinking

The more precise you can be as a mentor in creating these key moments, the more effective you can be.

The difficulty that we need to overcome as a mentor is that, more and more, we are living in a culture of immediate information and instant gratification. "Just tell me the answer!"

In some contexts, people become outraged by being asked to think, reflect, and draw their own conclusions. However, if you allow the frustration to continue until the penny drops, lessons learnt in this way will stick for ever. When we are lucky enough to have a real 'ah-ha' moment, we own it; it becomes our own revelation, not some semi-useful bit of advice that can be forgotten within six months.

If mentees engage in this game of raising the bar and learning on a deeper level they will find it so much more rewarding. Communicating clearly, expediently and effectively may be extremely successful in many types of activities, not just for mentoring.

In our efforts to communicate with clarity we make the message unengaging and allow the listener to give it no deep thought. If I were to deliver a speech and at the end, there were no questions, then I would be concerned.

My friend Daryll has a particular way of getting his kids to engage in activities. To try to sell it to them, or to force them to engage, doesn't work. Instead, he will begin doing the activity (playing the game or drawing the picture) and wait until the kids get curious... Then when they approach and ask to join in, he doesn't let them, only when they persist does he then let them join in and then they join in with their full attention.

Throughout this book, I will provide MENTORING techniques and something about the spirit of delivering them. (Generally, if the technique is delivered in a judgmental or 'factual' way (you should X, or what you need to do is Y), it will be met with resistance and it won't work.

All you need to dive into mentoring in this way is an unswervingly positive intention for the person you are mentoring and the playful flexibility of a favourite grandparent in how you communicate with them.

In August 1995, the World Diving Cup had just finished and the whole team were waiting at the airport to travel home from Atlanta. It was exactly a year before the 1996 Olympic Games and we had just finished competing in the pool that would host the diving for those games. I'd done okay; actually, pretty well for a 17-year-old on the GB men's team.

I was so excited. I'd just had my first experience of a major diving championship, since I'd just missed out on the Commonwealth Games the year before. This was a new level of performance now that I was on the senior team.

Filled with excitement and anticipation, I was getting closer to my dream of competing at the Olympic Games. I said aloud: 'This place is amazing – the pool has almost an electric atmosphere. I'm tingling all over. I can't wait to come back next year to the Olympic Games." I said with all the enthusiasm of a child with a dream: "It's already Olympic-tastic. Imagine what it'll be like when we come back."

Mentor

The head coach of British Diving, whom I respected and looked up to as a mentor, heard my comments and, without a moment of hesitation, looked me dead in the eye and, in front of the whole team, he said: "You're not good enough to qualify for the Olympic Games."

At the time, I had no idea what to make of that statement. To be honest, I thought that he was probably just tired and being a git. However, what he was doing was actually quite clever.

Now I'm certainly not suggesting that you deliver challenges in exactly this way.

What I am saying is that for me (and for some other high-performers I know who have had similar experiences), this was a catalyst for a leap in motivation. I was tormented by his words; and it wasn't the first or last time that I would be tormented by a mentor.

In that moment I made a decision... I would be going to the Olympic Games in 1996. "I'll show you who's not good enough to go to the Olympic Games."

I qualified for the Olympic games the following year and I'm really proud that I managed to achieve it at the same time as passing my A levels.

My good friend Colin Jackson tells a great story of being tormented by his mentor, Daley Thompson.

Colin won silver at the 1988 Olympic Games in the 110m hurdles and was really chuffed. He'd made it, so off he went to Daley's room to show his medal to his hero. Daley glanced at the medal and said; "I didn't know they made Olympic medals in that colour."

This tongue-in-cheek comment from Daley drove Colin on to become one of the UK's most successful athletes, winning multiple titles and setting many world records along the way.

What is MENTORING?

So, if you are with me, and you agree that great mentoring communication is more playful than immediate problem-solving or being efficient and direct, then you may be wondering how you get away with it. There are conditions/ ground rules that will need to exist between the mentor and mentee for my approach to be most effective.

MENTOR Technique: **Setting it up**

1. Attention

In relation to mentoring conversations; ask yourself if you have their full attention. Have they dedicated a reasonable amount of time for a conversation? Probably most importantly, are they valuing the interaction highly enough? This is of course a subjective appraisal, and each mentor-mentee relationship has a different dynamic.

If the attention frame isn't met – and that's okay, we all get busy – simply invite them to come back when they are less distracted. Be aware that attempting to discipline them is likely to damage the relationship. Relationships work best when both parties want to be there!

2. Intention

If you wish to get buy-in, and a move towards a more challenging, supportive and rewarding mentoring relationship, it's important to be clear about intentions. As a general rule, we usually evaluate communication from a perspective of:

What's in it for me?: Why should I? What am I expected to do? How can I? What if I do?

As a perfect starting point, it's those unspoken questions that you need to answer. As a mentor, if you are open and clear about your intentions for the mentee, they will not forget 'whose side you are on?' or 'where you are coming from?' This is especially important when you're challenging their thinking or behaviour.

An example would be: "My intention is to help you become aware of where you might not be helping yourself, so, to do that, I may ask some challenging questions. Please don't feel you need to justify anything to me – the purpose of the question is to get you to really think/reflect on what you are saying."

Another example, if they were taking themselves too seriously, would be: "My intention is to help you become aware of where you are not helping yourself by getting stressed. To do this, I'm more than likely to make light of things that you think are a problem or even tease you a little bit. (If you choose this approach, then it's important that you do so affectionately, with a twinkle in the eye.)

When you challenge, tease or tell a story to someone you are mentoring, they need to be applying it to themselves; becoming mindful of their own processes and behaviour, not deflecting it by turning their attention to you or your behaviour, which happens if the rapport is broken.

3. Expectation

It can be extremely effective to set some ground rules, but it's the mentee who should be the one taking responsibility for getting the value from the relationship. Although it's worth pointing out that, when the relationship is in full swing, set up correctly and working effectively, it will be extremely rewarding to both parties.

If you as the mentor are attempting to sell it to them, or convince them of the value of your input, then the relationship is not going to be effective.

One simple way of getting them to take responsibility is to provide them with choice. A great way to do this is make the options as real as possible through storytelling. It makes it indirect and engaging, and the choice becomes so much easier. Here's an example:

"When I was younger, I had to make a choice between two mentors that I had worked with in the past. They were very different. One was really helpful; I would tell him/her what was bothering me at the time and he/she would provide a really helpful suggestion – an immediate fix. It was very efficient. I asked a question, got a great answer, didn't need to think much, just did what he/she said, and that was it. I struggle to find an example now. I can't really remember anything he/she told me, but it was great at the time.

The other one was much more frustrating. I just wanted to find an answer to my question, a quick fix, but he/she would never give me straightforward advice – it was really frustrating. He/She would ask me questions that really made me think and sometimes I didn't get it until the next day, or sometimes even longer. He/She would tell stories that were really interesting but seemed a bit off-topic. But the funny thing is that I remember them – I remember so many of his/her little phrases and life lessons and when I look back now, they made a massive difference.

If you were in my shoes, which would you have chosen?

There is no point starting until you have had a great chat about the conversations you will be having.

Enjoy taking your time and discussing how to set it up; it's the most important step in the relationship.

Decisions, decisions...

Any journey begins with a decision, and there are many important decisions taken along the way, which, in retrospect, you realise were important crossroads and milestones.

> ***Committed decisions are probably the most important decisions you will ever make.***

I remember watching the Olympic Games on the TV in 1984. I was nearly seven and driving my parents mad with my endless energy. I constantly craved attention and spent most of my time bouncing off the walls. I was into sport by this time; it was my parents' clever way of tiring me out. I was already into swimming and gymnastics and would try any sport my parents would take me to. I loved being active.

I was captivated by the Olympic Games – there were so many sports people from countries I had never heard of, and sports I'd never even seen. It was probably one of the few times I would sit down. (Sit down, not sit still.)

I have one very vivid memory of those games. It is of watching one of the all-time greats, Daley Thompson, receiving his Olympic gold medal. He stood tall on the podium as the Union Jack was being raised slowly to 'God Save the Queen', and he was whistling. Daley had just successfully defended his Olympic title in the decathlon. I didn't really know who he was or what he had achieved; however, I was glued to the screen, fascinated. I asked my dad, somewhat confused, why this man was whistling? My dad told me that he was trying to stop himself crying. "Crying?" I exclaimed. "Why is he crying? He's won the gold?" I couldn't understand why he would want to cry..... I only cried when I got beaten. My father said: "Well, Leon, when people are really, really happy they sometimes cry. Daley Thompson is that happy. Because, Leon, as a sports person, there is nothing greater than the Olympic Games."

My response was: "I want to go, I want to go, I want to go." It must have seemed crazy for a six-year-old to think of going to the Olympic Games, but I really had made a decision.

I think nearly everyone who makes it to the Olympic Games has had one of these moments real decision. My friend, Steve Backley, Britain's greatest-ever javelin thrower, tells a captivating story of his feelings of inspired awe watching "the gladiators on the TV screen" during the 1976 Olympic Games.

Any achievement begins with a decision; the decision to commit, to go for it, to be bold enough to go for it whole-heartedly and not to downscale your ambitions at the first bit of negative feedback. Only when you look back in time from a position of having achieved your goal, will you see these decisions as important crossroads and milestones.

This applies as much to everyday life as it does to Olympic performance – the decision to go for the job you want; to start your own business; to start a home-study course; to go after someone to whom you're attracted.

Your role as a mentor is to encourage people into clarity and action by provoking congruent decisions: to set the goal; raise the bar; go after the prize; (and to alert them when they lack conviction or commitment).

After all, not making a decision is a decision. It's the decision to do nothing.

I promise that, if you can encourage people to leave behind the vague world of half-decision and underperformance, you are helping them to take the bold, first steps towards a higher level of achievement.

"There's a difference between interest and commitment. When you're interested in doing something, you do it only when it's convenient. When you're committed to something, you accept no excuses; only results"
Kenneth Blanchard

As a mentor, it helps to be aware of the things that indicate half-decisions and cop-outs so you can question them.

MENTOR technique: **Trying and shoulding**

There are a couple of words that can alert you that someone is being indecisive, or indicate that someone is choosing to fall short of the task in advance:

"Try"

Consider the difference between the following two sentences:

- I will go to the gym tonight
- I will try to go to the gym tonight

What's going on with the speaker that would lead them to use the second statement?

In order for the word, "try" to pop up the speaker needs a feeling of uncertainty, or needs to be paying attention to something that could prevent it from happening.

"Should"

Again, consider the difference between the following two sentences:

- I'm going to the gym tonight
- I should go to the gym tonight

The word "should" can have two underlying meanings. It could be a loose estimate with plenty of uncertainty: "All being well, I should be there." (This is a very similar thought process to "try".)

Or it could be a decision to fail in advance: "I should be there (but I won't)." This often indicates a feeling of obligation – but obligation does not make things happen. The will and decision to act does. Obligation just costs energy, so anything you can do to clear their path of obligation and get them to commit to decisions will help their performance.

There are several ways that you can challenge these thought patterns. In doing so, the intention of the mentor is to encourage them to be realistic, help them to free themselves of obligations, and push them to be more decisive.

Examples of what to do with someone who is "trying":
Statement: "I will try to go to the gym tonight."
Response 1: Direct challenge: "OK, just level with me, will you go or not? It's OK either way, let's just be clear about it."
Response 2: Misunderstand: "Ok; so you are saying it doesn't matter if you go or not?" (this will provoke more clarity)
Response 3: Find the obstacle: "What could get in the way?"

The same challenges can be effective with someone who is "shoulding":
Statement: "I really should go to the gym tonight"
Response 1: Direct Challenge: "OK; if you are not going to, don't kid yourself. So let's be clear: are you going to go or not?"

Response 2: Misunderstand: "OK; so you're saying that you are not bothered about fitness?"
Response 3: Find the obstacle: "What prevents you from going? Who says you should go?"

By the way: if the 'should' is a guilty feeling, what arrangements do they need to make so that they can free themselves of the feeling of obligation and get on with their performance? I'm sure you'll agree, that feeling you "should" be doing something and beating yourself up because you're not doing it, doesn't help.

I have lost count of the number of birthdays and special occasions I chose to miss when training for the Olympic Games. They are tough choices, imagine missing your best friend's 21st birthday or your girlfriend's grandfather's funeral. This obviously really affected me, so I would have a sulk for a short time but then I accepted it and got on with what I had to do, if I spent the whole time dwelling on it, then I may as well have been at the event because I wouldn't be getting what I needed from the training.

There is, of course, a pay-off to not making a decision or committing to something – it means that you don't have to do it. For many of us, we are programmed to avoid discomfort, which leads us to take the path of least resistance or not stretch ourselves. It's very efficient, and may allow you to be chilled out, but staying firmly in the comfort zone is not very rewarding and certainly doesn't create opportunity for those moments of extraordinary performance. As a mentor, if you think that someone is well within their comfort zone, gently pushing them toward decisions, commitments and raising the bar will help them enormously.

Well-intentioned terrorists

I coined this phrase while studying Business & Finance at Sheffield Hallam University in 2006. I was reading about how some customers, if not treated well, can become terrorists as they share their negative experience with other potential customers and scare them off.

It struck a chord with me at the time because I was doing my best to ignore scary scenarios from the people around me; and they were trying to help!

Imagine the scene: you are in the zone,. You have controlled everything within your control, and forgotten about everything out of your control; you have visualised your perfect performance; you have a comfortable belief in your ability. Anything less than excellent is not on your radar. You are determined and you are in a state of physical high-performance. Then, someone close to you says:

"Well, I don't suppose it matters. You've done well to get this far haven't you? Are you sure that you're ready? Have you seen the size of the crowd? You look nervous; are you okay? We believe in you, you won't let us down will you? Just go for gold! Don't think about the last competition where you messed up. Have you seen how well he is/they are performing? I know you won't let us down!"

Well-intentioned terrorists are those who do not mean any harm but can cause the most damage to performance.

There have been many occasions where it wasn't the opposition or the magnitude of the competition that threw me off my game, but someone close, who was trying to help with words of encouragement. I had one particular coach with whom I really struggled because his every input was a critique. His heart was in the right place but he would tell me what not to do or only what I was doing wrong. This made me really self-conscious and dented my confidence. I found it so frustrating. "I know what I'm doing wrong. Please tell me what to do instead! Give me solutions, please!"

Using negative language is not just using unhelpful words; it's what you're actually paying attention to.

As you read this paragraph, don't think of baked beans. How are you getting on with that? How about not thinking of the Apple logo or not thinking of the sound your computer makes when you turn it on?

When you use a negative, you are introducing the very thing that you are attempting to avoid and therefore drawing direct attention to it.

What happens when you start a conversation with, "Don't worry..." or "It's nothing to worry about... " The response could be, "I wasn't worried until you said 'don't worry' and now I'm wondering if I should be worried." You are accidently introducing the idea of worrying.

MENTOR technique: **Flip it back to the positive**

Statement: What I don't want to happen is...

Mentoring Response: So what do you want to happen?

Statement: It's not that....

Mentoring Response: Isn't it? Why mention it then? What is it?

Statement: I can't do anything about it!

Mentoring Response: So what can you do something about?

Statement: It won't work!

Mentoring Response: So what will work?

You hear athletes talk frequently about having positive mental attitude. This is not simply: "Be optimistic and you will do great" (although that does help).

It's about being mindful of what you are focusing on. Where is your attention going?

Is your attention on what you do want to happen? Or is your attention on what you don't want to happen?

Because whichever way you look, that's what you will get more of.

One of the best examples of this is a psychological experiment conducted by Robert Rosenthal and Lenore Jacobson, who set out to investigate the effects of teachers' expectancies on the intelligence test scores of their pupils.

In this experiment, teachers were given false information about the learning potential of certain students. They were told that some randomly selected students had been tested and found to be on the brink of a period of rapid intellectual growth. When evaluated five, eight and twenty months later, the students exhibited increased performance on IQ tests. Their scores were way above what would normally have been expected of them.

They concluded that students' intellectual development is largely a response to what teachers expect and how those expectations are communicated. Teacher expectations can increase or decrease intelligence (IQ) test scores. This is referred to as "The Pygmalion Effect" or "self-fulfilling prophecy". The concept is beautifully simple: if we expect that something will happen, we behave (unconsciously) in a manner that will make it happen.

So the trick here is to positively corrupt expectations, ie direct attention to what can be done (not what can't) and then expect it to go well. You will be amazed at the results for those who you mentor.

Well-intentioned terrorists

So how can you comment on performance without being critical and focusing on the negative?

The answer is simple – reinforce the positive and do it again, and again, and again.

For example, if a child attempts to write a word and spells it incorrectly, rather than you making a big red cross that is likely to provoke an unhelpful reaction, acknowledge the elements that they have done correctly and ask them to do it again.

The traditional approach would be:

Skool ✗

I was recently on a workshop with someone who had been studying the work of Dr. Tony Humphreys, and he offers a more helpful way of providing guidance:

S k o o l

✔ _ ✔ ✔ ✔ nearly there...

People generally try to improve performance by pointing out mistakes or errors. It's how we have become accustomed to evaluating everything. Take a moment to evaluate the sentence overleaf:

Mentor

"If you think you cando a thing or think you carnt do a thing, you're right." Henry Ford

If I were to ask you to comment on it, the first thing you are likely to say is, "There's a typo (or two)!"

I bet your first thought was "that's wrong!" – and while you were fixating on the error you may have missed some of the positives such as: "how interesting?"; "great bit of wisdom"; or "nice font".

It's a challenge to notice and reinforce the positive; we are generally too busy being critical as mistakes leap out at us.

Let's imagine interacting with someone who sometimes does something that is unhelpful and at other times doesn't. The general approach is to make them aware of what they are doing that's unhelpful and then tell them to stop or change it.

When you draw attention to a problem, the person may have no idea what to do instead. It's very difficult to just stop doing something. It is easy to do something else instead.

A far more effective approach would be to make them aware when they are performing well and say, "Great – more of that, please."

***"Few things in the world are more powerful than a positive push. A smile. A word of optimism and hope. A 'you can do it' when things are tough"
Richard M. De Vos***

To sum up: The fastest and most helpful approach to encouraging development, nurturing talent, and raising the bar is: ***Expect people to do well and reinforce the positive rather than criticising the negative.***

More of what you do want – not less of what you don't!

MENTOR technique **"If it ain't broke, don't create it"**

As I mentioned earlier, the mentee needs to be in the right state of mind for the mentoring communication to be effective. As with all communication, it's a two-way-street so the mentor also needs to be in the right frame of mind. ***The number-one quality of great mentor is the ability to really listen, patiently, carefully and with a curious, open mind.***

As a mentor, you need to be very careful not to try to fix a problem that the mentee doesn't have. It's just that you may have found it tricky once upon a time. I've had to stop myself on many occasions from sharing my problems that I managed to fix in the past, ones that Tom doesn't have. This doesn't serve Tom; it brings into his awareness something that isn't his problem. As the saying goes, "If it ain't broke, don't fix it!" I need to respond to what I'm seeing and hearing as opposed to what I imagine might be going on or what I think I would find difficult – he's not me!

For example, if a diver says "I'm having trouble with this dive", there are lots of meanings I could attach to that:

- They are performing the dive and not getting what they view to be a good result.

Well-intentioned terrorists

Well, I think that it is safe to assume this from what they said.

What may **not** be safe to assume is:

- They are scared of it
- They don't think they can do it
- They are having a bad day
- They are being negative
- They are having a confidence wobble
- They haven't been practising
- They are having trouble on the (a) take off (b) flight (c) entry to water (whichever one I found difficult when I performed it).

It's so easy to find yourself thinking things like this, but we have no reason to think in this way, based on anything other than our own expectations or perceptions. You need to ask exactly how they are having trouble with it, rather than guessing.

I suggest that you work only with what they give you – don't impose solutions to problems they haven't got. It's an exercise in listening and going with what they give you – rather than basing it on your expectations.

"The greatest good you can do for another is not just to share your riches but to reveal to him his own" Benjamin Disraeli

Mentor

If a diver says: "I'm having trouble with this dive", I remind myself that I have no idea what that means and ask a question to specify the problem:

- How are you having trouble specifically?
- What exactly are you having trouble with?

You can begin to help only when you have a more specific description of the problem.

It's important to remember, as illustrated by the Rosenthal Experiment in the previous chapter. If you assume that he/she is having a problem you may impose that difficulty or limitation on them through your own behaviour and language. To be a great mentor, you need to see the potential in the person you are working with and believe that, whatever their current performance, they are ultimately capable of achieving their goal.

If you don't believe that, then I suggest that you either find a way of changing your own mind or encourage them to find another mentor because you won't be doing them any favours by going through the motions.

The Leon Nod. (Advanced mentoring technique)

I have a behaviour, a very natural one, that I was previously unaware of doing, until it was named 'the Leon Nod' by those around me! I tend to give people choices while nodding enthusiastically – this has an interesting effect as people respond more to the nod than they do to the words, allowing me to raise the bar swiftly instead of talking someone round slowly. As per the Rosenthal psychology experiment, so much of our influence and encouragement comes from our unconscious non-verbal communication.

What's it all about?

Sydney Olympic Games, 2000, men's 10m synchronised diving final – the German pair of Jan Hempel and Heiko Meyer hit the water on their final dive, Peter and I hold our breath; they were slightly out of time, weren't they? Differing angles of entry; surely the judges are going to mark them accordingly? Surely we will be Olympic bronze medallists. Surely?

Fourth place is the worst place to finish in any event and at an Olympic Games, it is no less than devastating. You feel drained, deflated, frustrated, upset, angry to name but a few of the gazillion emotions that zip around your body. I had trained so hard, six hours a day, six days a week, totalling around 7,500 hours of training in the four-year Olympic cycle, for this, this moment. Stood on the pool deck, illuminated by the dazzling TV lights, surrounded by the noise of 18,000 spectators who were thrilled by the contest they just witnessed, I'm in top physical condition, I should be on top of the world, but instead I'm broken.

Fourth place is so difficult to accept, especially when it's people's opinion deciding your fate and whether you realise your dream or not. You're at the mercy of the judges in a subjective sport. It's not like Wimbledon, where the computer can tell you if the ball is in or out and if you do come fourth, you still get paid loads of money and can come back the next year to give it another go! Four years is a lifetime in a sport like diving, and there is no money to be made. Did I want to do another four years of six hours a day, six days a week of blood, sweat and tears? Did I want to make all those sacrifices again? Was it worth it?

I remember being on interviewed on the poolside in Sydney, by Sharron Davies. The first question she asked was 'so the judging seemed awful,: "You were clearly robbed of an Olympic medal – what do you think of the judges?"

Great question. Somehow my media training cut in; I chose not to answer emotively and get my big blame finger out, instead I said.

What's it all about?

"You know what, the judging is the judging. We can't control that – it's the nature of the sport. But I tell you one thing: we will be back in four years to challenge again for the medals."

So it started again, the four-year cycle, in which I would total around 7,500 hours of training in pursuit of my dream. There were so many sacrifices to be made, so many variables to account for and so many plans to set in motion. Any athlete will tell you how tough an Olympic cycle is; how many ups and downs there are. Nothing ever runs completely to plan. It's a rollercoaster at best! That said, it's so important to have plans. How else would you know where you're going? You wouldn't set sail without any idea of where you're going and which direction you need to go in order to get there. Sport is all about having a plan and setting goals. Short-, medium- and long-term goals are set up in a 'periodised training plan' that shows everything from the exact day that you are aiming to peak in your performance, right down to the number of reps on a particular exercise on a particular training day.

You can imagine how this level of planning becomes a habit in every area of your life when you're an elite athlete. I remember being with my mum, dad and younger sister Nadine on our first family holiday for 20 years (a career in Olympic sport means you miss out on many family holidays). We were travelling around the amazing and beautiful British Columbia in Canada. I was sitting in the driver's seat of our hire car feeling very excited about the day ahead. There was so much to take in, and I felt extremely lucky to be sharing it with my family. I turned to my dad, who on this occasion was co-pilot, and said,

"What's the plan, dad?"

To which my dad responded: "There is no plan." This did not compute so I said, "Of course, you need a plan, dad – don't be silly!"

"Well Leon, if you don't have a plan then nothing can go wrong"

I was nearly crying with laughter. I said to my dad that if I ever wrote a book, I would share his words of wisdom.

Setbacks are sometimes life's greatest gifts. Saying that, I've never met anyone who thinks that in the moment that a setback happens, especially when it's of significant size and enough to put you on your backside. We've all been there, I'm sure. Setbacks are not in the plan, but they always occur, most likely at the most inconvenient time too.

In April 1998, to get the judge's attention and change the perception of British diving, I set myself the challenge of inventing the world's most difficult dive; I had it planned out in my head, I'd visualised what it was going to be like; and I'd diligently broken the dive down into its parts and practiced them all. So imagine my surprise when the first time I attempted it, I hit the water at a strange angle and almost left my right arm behind.

From that day forward, my shoulder was knackered. It scrunched, it scraped, and there was a shooting pain every time I moved it. I was determined and bloody-minded enough to carry on and keep "toughing it out" for almost three years, before deciding that enough was enough and maybe it was about time I stopped being so tough. The qualities of tenacity and determination can lead you to some dark places physically. I know many athletes who will never give up; this is where you need those around you to keep an eye on you and make sure that you don't push yourself too far.

I needed reconstructive shoulder surgery on my right shoulder. The doctors suggested that I had a 40% chance of making it back to my current level of diving. I would be in rehabilitation for six months and in a sling for 24 hours a day for the first four weeks - nice!

I faced the biggest challenge of my life. Six months of rehab to make it back into the pool and start low-level diving again, with no guarantees that I would make it back at all. It was as if I'd lost everything that I'd worked so hard to achieve. If I were to get it back, I needed to let go of where I was (GB number one) and start from where I now found myself (in a sling unable to move my arm).

In order to get back into the pool, I had to follow a new plan, forgetting about the 2001 World Championships and setting my sights on first getting back into the pool and then aiming to qualify for 2002 Commonwealth Games.

It was the toughest journey of my life. I visited some dark places along the way, but I made it back into the pool and began low-level diving ahead of schedule. I'd proved them wrong again, or so I thought.

Yet something wasn't quite right; my shoulder was better but not fixed. There was still a scrunching feeling and as a result, it couldn't quite do what I needed it to do. My progress in the pool started to grind to a halt. So off I went back to see the specialists to get some reassurance.

Instead, I was told that I needed another surgery, as unfortunately for me, the first surgical intervention hadn't worked as well as they had hoped it would. It was bad enough the first time when I had time to recover, but now it was November 2001. I was back under the surgeon's knife for another operation, and time was running out for me to get back.

If I didn't compete for GB that coming competitive season (only a few months away), then my funding would be stopped and I would be off the team. Dream over, no Olympic medal, game over. The pressure was really on, screwing me down into the floor.

So I threw everything and the kitchen sink at my recovery and mission to get back to international competition standard. I set tougher goals, made even more sacrifices and became completely obsessive in my behaviour. I was focused, determined and tenacious. I was using all the behaviours that got me to the top, so why was nothing working? Why was everything going wrong?

Mentor

Why did I hate my life? Why was this happening to me? I was in a really bad place to put it mildly. I felt like I was at the bottom of a muddy ditch and all I needed to do was get out. But every time I would scramble up the bank and almost get to the top, digging my fingers in, I would slip all the way back down. ***Something was missing.***

I was in Seville in Spain, competing for GB at the World Diving Cup. I'd just about scraped into the team. It was seven months since my second shoulder operation and I had just put in a poor performance. Everything had reached breaking point and I was on the poolside in tears; I had no idea what to do. This is when my mentor came quietly over and rather than trying to fix the problem or give me advice, he placed his hand on my shoulder and asked me a question: "Why do you do this sport, Leon?"

So I blurted out a reply: "Because I enjoy it".

"So why haven't I seen you smile for six months?" That was the ah-ha moment, the moment that the penny dropped, like a clash of thunder right in between my ears. Of course, that was it: what had been missing; the real reason why I chose to do this sport; and the reason I had been doing it every day since I was eight years old; because I enjoyed it.

Enjoyment, for me, is the key ingredient to success. No wonder I was stuck at the bottom of that ditch and nothing was working, I was trying to perform at the highest level without my biggest emotive driver.

I returned home to the UK and went to my first training session putting on a big fat smile of my face. By the end of the session, it wasn't so much of an effort to hold the smile, and by the end of the week, my smile was 100% genuine. The negative spiral I had caught myself in had reversed into a positive spiral. I was finally out of the ditch. It's amazing how quickly things can turn around; if you change your physiology you change the thought patterns in your brain.

Only five weeks later I was back at the top of my game and won a silver medal at the Commonwealth Games in Manchester in one of the closest and most exciting competitions in the history of diving. Having more than 2,000 people stamping their feet, clapping their hands and chanting your name before you dive is a truly unbelievable experience and was a long way from standing on that poolside in tears just five weeks earlier.

MENTOR technique: **What's it all about?**

As a performer, we can become lost in the overwhelming complexity and intensity of our short-term goals. When we're in this state, we occasionally have moments of clarity, but these are few and far between, especially when we are stressed or performing beyond capacity. Sound familiar?

At times like this, a mentor can remind us of our values and driving intentions, bringing us back to what is most important, by asking a "what's it all about?" style question. It's one of the most impactful things a great mentor can do – because they have the perspective to lift people out of the detail of the day and check that they are steering the ship in the right direction.

There are several questions that work quite nicely:

What are you doing this for?
What's your intention?
What's important to you about... ?
What's the purpose of... ?
What do you want to get from... ?

You can fill in the '...?' with the activity you are discussing at the time.

In doing so, you are moving the person's attention to a higher level (more general and more abstract) to avoid being lost in the day-to-day churn.

Sometimes, in my experience of facilitating workshops, I may ask someone what they want to achieve and it's not uncommon that they don't have a clear idea.

Whether you are reminding someone of their intentions or awakening an awareness of intentions for the first time, it's a fantastic question to ask. When someone is aware of his or her intentions, values or emotive drivers, then they can check out if their current behaviour is getting them what they want.

To put it simply; ***if what you are doing is not in line with your real intentions, then it's time to change something.***

Note: Here's something to watch out for when asking people about their intentions. ***Real intentions are succinct***. They are rarely more than a few words. They are emotive drivers and, as such, do not generally have lengthy descriptions.

Long sentences are usually explanations, rationalisations or justifications. If you ask someone's intention and they give you a media sound-bite, a load of management speak, or something that sounds like a mission statement, then it might be what they are thinking but it's not the driving intention.

Mentor

I often find that when I'm working with athletes who spend time in the spotlight, their barriers can remain up most of the time; it's a default setting from their media training.

Some athletes are especially good at saying the right thing at the right time. As a mentor (without a hidden agenda), it is your role to be patient, to ask a question again and maybe to reassure them of where you're going with it, in order to allow the barriers to lower.

If they reply to the question with a long-winded statement, then simply smile and ask, "And what's the intention in that?" or "And what's important to you about that?" and so on.

By asking the same question twice, you will get closer to what it's really about.

You can then go on to ask if they are achieving their intention, and if not, what can they do differently?

What exactly is the problem?

Peter Waterfield and I are great mates and we have been friends since we were kids. Over the 15 amazing years we spent together as synchronised diving partners and competing against each other, we enjoyed many ups and downs and shared a common desire; to be the best we could be at this crazy sport of diving. During my competitive career, Pete was a friend first and a business partner second.

We would always room together when we were on GB duty and we had such a laugh all of the time. We've been to some amazing places around the globe, stayed in some fantastic hotels and some real dives (excuse the pun) too! Whether we were staying in a freezing cold, bare box room in northern Germany or in a luxurious five-star hotel room in Florida, we had fun, and lots of it. We were two great friends travelling the globe together and doing what we loved.

Early in our careers, we found ourselves aiming for Olympic qualification at the European Championships in Helsinki. It was June 2000. The Sydney Olympic Games were in the following September; such a stressful and exciting time 'setting out our stall' and trying to earn a spot at the Olympic Games.

Peter and I were fit, in shape and injury-free. The Europeans is highly contested, especially in both the men's 10m synchro and the 10m individual events. We were up against strong teams from Russia, Germany and Ukraine to name a few; a medal was possible and we needed to get everything right.

After the prelims, we were 4th. That was fine though, because the points did not carry through to the final; our performance was good enough for now and with a boost, we could raise our game in the final and earn a spot on the podium. We were really tired. It doesn't really get dark in Finland during June and we had paper-thin curtains in our room so we were struggling to sleep!

Mentor

After the prelim, we had time for lunch and a power nap before returning to the pool for the final in the evening. We were following "the plan" sticking to "the routine" and having fun.

I was waiting patiently for Pete, as I always did. He won't mind me saying that it was me who kept us on time. He was on the phone to his new girlfriend. She was 16 and he was 19 at the time; they had been together only a short time and things were going really well.

I became aware of Pete saying, "What's wrong, babe?" Please tell me, I know something's up. It doesn't matter what it is, just tell me." He repeated this several times. Even before I saw his face go from mild frustration to absolute shock, I somehow knew "what was up" as if there was a glitch in the matrix.

"Shit, I'm going to be a dad!" he said with the same expression as someone who's got to the top of the 10m board and forgotten to put on his Speedos. "What am I going to do?" Pete's head, quite understandably, was in a spin and we were about to miss the bus from the hotel to the pool to compete in the final of the European Championships! Woohoo!

I was thinking, *Panic stations! What can I do? We have to compete, we can't ask them to delay the competition in order for Pete can get his head around things. It's time to do something, anything.*

The conversation went something like this:

Pete: "My girlfriend's dad is going to kill me."

(I was thinking, "Yes, he probably is. He's dead! But it's not happening now, and we've got a medal to win.)

Me: "Yeah, maybe, I guess you just don't know. What I do know is there's nothing you can do about it until we get back."

We continued the conversation in which I empathised with his current situation, briefly talked through possible scenarios with their pros and cons and I was able to guide him back out of his spin. I first acknowled that his girlfriend's dad might want to kill him and other such understandable worries. I then became more specific about what we could do – all with one eye on the bus about to leave for the pool.

Me: "When do you actually need to deal with this? Do you need to decide what to do right now, or is it best to wait and discuss it face to face with Tania when you get home in a few days?"

Pete: (Still a bit shell-shocked) "Er, yeah, suppose you're right."

He quickly began to come around to what he could do right now and how that would help. So instead of endlessly mulling over all the options, he decided to "hold" or 'park' them until he returned home. He realised that one week would make no difference in the grand scheme of things.

Pete had to get back to the here-and-now. Once he had made the decision to wait until he was home to figure out the way forward, I was able to guide his attention and refocus on the job in hand. We were about to dive in the European Final. He decided to keep it simple and between us only. This was to prevent any helpful, well-intended advice or opinions coming from our teammates, which would have definitely put his head back into a spin.

I suggested that it was lucky that he had this diving competition to get stuck into and take his mind off things. He seemed to embrace that idea as a great escape from the drama and threw himself fully into the task at hand, challenging for a medal at the European Championships.

We won bronze. Pete and Tania are still together; they were married in 2007. Their fantastic little boy, Lewis Waterfield, was born in February 2001.

MENTOR Technique: **Get down to the specifics**

If people are overwhelmed with too many things at once, or if they become stressed, then they can often make a few problems into a catastrophe and say, "It's everything!"

"Nothing is particularly hard if you divide it into small jobs" - Henry Ford

Many distractions and problems are not happening right now. They are either something in the past that you are dwelling on and cannot change, or something in the future that may not even happen. The more you realise this, the easier it is to deal with it. When people are overwhelmed or freaking out – ***you can use specific questions to break the circumstances down into more manageable chunks.***

There are two questions that are the most effective for getting to the bottom of what's really going on: "What" questions and "How" questions. To answer them, you have to move your attention to a more specific level.

For example, if the person is saying and thinking, "It's all going wrong!" you can ask what specifically is going wrong, or how exactly is it going wrong.

What exactly is the problem?

When faced with a defeated statement such as "It won't work!" you can ask how will it not work, or what about it will not work.

When you are breaking problems apart by making them more specific, I suggest that you ***resist the temptation to ask 'Why?'*** Why not ask why? Because the answer to why is because.

If they are saying, "It's all going wrong," or "It won't work," if you ask 'why?' they will give you a reason or a list of reasons.

The question 'why?' invites explanations or justifications. It will take you round and round in circles, getting more and more understanding of circumstances but no specifics – There will be no details of what is actually happening.

During this questioning process, it's important to be non-confrontational (or else it will quickly become an argument).

Softly, softly

Generally speaking, if you are less assertive, it's easier to challenge effectively so that your mentee really takes it on board. (There are, of course, exceptions to this rule; sometimes, a short, sharp shock does wonders to provoke a step-change.) For the most part, if you have more of a 'take it or leave it' attitude, you are likely to bypass any knee-jerk resistance that would be provoked by being too direct. Besides, it's great if everything is the mentee's choice – they own the change.

So, as a mentor, it's good to use indirect conversational language: "I'm wondering... I'm just curious to know... it's interesting that..."

I don't know about you, but the moment someone says to me, "What you need to do Leon is... " I immediately stop listening and think, "Oh really! I'll be the judge of that, thank you very much!"

As mentors, we are steering and influencing as best we can, not telling. To achieve this, you need to be extremely clear that you are entirely on the side of the mentee and not judging them.

There is no point arguing with a mentee. You are likely to lose your influence because it's easier for them to deflect or resist your suggestions when you are having an argument.

Your job is to lead the horse to water, not to make it drink.

MENTOR Technique
Creating U-turns, not road blocks

Sometimes, the people whom you are communicating with will kick back. They may answer defensively, or even say something that seems like a counter-attack.

To overcome this and keep things going, there is a need to create U-turns, not road blocks. There are five examples of how to do this below:

As an example, imagine that I'm doing a corporate presentation, and someone says: "Your Olympic story is great, but it doesn't apply to my performance in business."

I can respond in a variety of ways:

1. Go with them then turn it around

"That's right. It's a metaphor; there's a need to examine the difference between my story and yours in order to apply it."

2. Go with them and exaggerate

I agree (with a cheeky smile): "I can't believe that I get paid for this. Why are you all here?"

3. Go with them, then discover a counter-example

Yeah. Although, from feedback and the conversations I have

at the end of these sessions, some people are able to take the messages from my story and apply them to their world.

4. Agree, then contradict with a story
Fair enough. I was working as an Olympic Ambassador for one organisation and I really questioned what my story had to do with their current initiatives, until one of their internal communications team said, "Your story is about raising performance and overcoming challenges, and that can be applied to everything."

5. Demonstrate agreement with your behaviour then contradict
OK... "The Leon Nod" and showing that you are taking their comment positively; and then after a few seconds of evaluation... I disagree.

Really? How do you know?

It's so hot in the balcony at Ponds Forge Aquatic Centre in Sheffield, especially when there is a competition taking place. I'm sure that management of the building aren't turning the heat up, but it certainly feels as if they are. The atmosphere at this time is electric; there is a buzz in the air, a competitive buzz. The whole building is filled with excitement and anticipation.

When it's competition time, you can really tell how people are doing. It's so interesting how different people react in the situation and either rise or fall to the occasion. When I was competing I used to be generally aware of other people's differing behaviour. Now that I'm a mentor, commentator and spectator, I'm fascinated.

One of the most enjoyable components when it comes to mentoring Tom is that we don't have a set mentoring time. For example, we don't meet once a week/month for a mentoring session. Ever since he was ten we have adopted the same approach. We keep in touch by occasional phone calls/ email/ Facebook and the most important times are always the face-to-face catch-ups. It never feels any different. I'm always mentoring and this allows me to intervene there and then if needs be rather than having to wait for, say, a set formal session. In fact, some of my best mentoring has happened in the most unlikely of settings.

Four of us sat there, chatting as the competition unfolded. It wasn't the most exciting event of the weekend; the 1m board is tough, but it is just not that high so it's never going to be as enthralling as the other diving events. Toina, Brooke, Tom and I sat there putting the world to rights. We were four friends, part-watching the competition and generally having a laugh.

I can't really remember exactly what we were talking about. It was a relaxed conversation: who's doing what; holidays; the weather; and so on!

Mentor

It was as we looked forward to the international diving competition calendar and who was diving in which competitions that I noticed an unusual change in Tom's language. He was talking about the events coming up, but not in his usual upbeat manner. He was focusing on "having to defend titles" and frequently mentioning "pressure". This set off alarm bells in my head; these patterns in his language were new.

I was picking up on his fear of not continuing to perform. It's perfectly normal to feel this once you've reached the top. My concern was that he didn't stay here for too long, as he could get stuck.

It is our successes that can limit us, not necessarily our failures.

As an everyday example I have a couple of friends from the world of business who describe a similar scenario. A creative entrepreneur with nothing to lose can achieve amazing things, creating new and adventurous services, breaking from the norm, taking risks, getting noticed, constantly over stretching themselves and delivering. However, once this young creative entrepreneur becomes a successful established entrepreneur, they may become risk-adverse – to protect what they have achieved and not upset the apple cart. They are in the prison of identity called "success" and will try to stay in that very comfortable prison at all costs. In such cases, the adventurous spirit that made them successful disappears completely and the success becomes harder and harder to maintain.

I asked Tom if he could name anyone in diving who had ever successfully defended all their titles? Asked as if I was pondering the question myself. He of course couldn't. I then casually asked if he could think of anyone in any sport, tennis, golf, and so on who successfully defended all their titles. I was letting him ponder and answer, never telling or lecturing him.

After we failed to come up with any names, I said: "The interesting thing for me is that these champions have learned what it takes to get all the way to the top and also what it is like to go back down. They then have the experience of both directions that gives them everything they need to hit the top when it matters. Well, I suppose that is what makes them so inspirational and true champions."

I then asked in a very indirect way: "So, what processes got you to the top? What did you focus on? I'm guessing those will serve you well again? What do you think?" I was watching Tom process and reflect.

We landed on the old favourites: focus on having fun; enjoy your diving; and the results will take care of themselves. This is the process that worked for me, and its what enabled Tom to become World Champion at 15. It's the attitude that is most likely to ensure he has many future successes.

Another conversation started with a call from Tom's coach. It's always good to build strong relationships with those close to the mentee as they can give you the heads-up when challenges are on the horizon.

Tom was building up to learn the world's most difficult dive and during the process, the wheels had come off slightly. Itß had started to affect his other dives; he was getting lost after taking off and not always performing the dive he was intending to. This can be quite common in diving, sometimes referred to as "lost move syndrome".

Golfers sometimes get it. It's called the 'yips'; an example is when a golfer goes for a short putt and instead of a controlled 'tap', they give it a whack. A darts player can also experience this 'LM syndrome'. When the player goes to throw the dart, they don't let go of it, almost as if it's stuck to their fingers. It sounds quite funny, but if you earn your keep through these activities, it's an awful experience.

I struggled with "lost move syndrome" a few times during my career, one of which I will never forget. I was in Sweden in a practice session just before competing in the European Diving Cup. The pool was packed with all the best teams in Europe, practising and fine-tuning their dives for the competition ahead.

I was performing one of the world's most dangerous dives (standing forwards on the 10m platform, jumping away from it and then spinning backwards towards the platform through 3.5 somersaults), in synchro with Peter Waterfield. As we took off from the board together, I got completely disorientated, panicked and then, like a rabbit in front of the headlights, I froze.

Instead of completing the dive as Pete did, I stayed in the tuck position and hit the water in a sitting position with my legs split, Speedos first at nearly 40 mph. I can't tell you how much that hurt but I'm sure that most of the guys who are reading this are already cringing. I hauled myself to the side and noticed the whole pool had come to a standstill, staring at me in silence. It's like a car crash; it's terrible but people can't help staring.

I was in a world of physical and emotional pain and immediately hobbled off to the men's changing room to check my bits and pieces were all intact. Fortunately, to my surprise and delight, everything was in order and once I had stopped feeling sick, it was decision time. Do I get back on the horse? Or do I wait? Do I procrastinate? Nobody would have blamed me for resting and waiting until the next day to get back in the pool; I'd just really hurt myself. However the voice in my head was warning me, "The longer you leave it, the harder it gets."

It's a long way up to the 10m board, feeling scared after a painful wipeout. I could feel the tension in the pool; all eyes were on me and seemed to be nervous for me.. Will he wipe out again?

I surfaced to a standing ovation with whistling and clapping from everyone in the pool, even though this was not a competition dive. I had absolutely nailed it; I would have been awarded 9.5s and 10s if it were being judged in competition. I'd got back on the horse.

When I struggled with 'lost move syndrome' it was contributed to by a loss of confidence. I was worrying about things out of my control, putting additional pressure on my self, getting myself in **a** right state, as opposed to **the** right state.

As a mentor, it's important to look for cause rather than just addressing symptoms. Coaches and people around me attempted to remind me of how to perform the dive and the technical adjustments to make (like, "let go at the right time, you doughnut, and stop landing on your bum"). But knowing how to do it wasn't the problem – I had done it hundreds of times. I needed help with my confidence.

So, Tom was getting himself in a state; worrying about attempting the world's most difficult dive. It was negatively affecting his performance on all dives. He was starting to get frustrated and anxious, and his general confidence was breaking down. We had a huge advantage as mentor and mentee because I invented the dive ten years before; so if anyone should be handing out tips and pointers, I was well qualified!

At the point when I intervened, he hadn't attempted the dive. He'd only been doing the build-ups. The dive is broken down into a series of stepping stones, each part added to the next eventually culminating in the full dive from the 10m board, so the 'problem' stemmed from his perception of what he was going to attempt rather than an experience of something he had attempted. Most people in the diving world would reinforce the belief that it's difficult, but how do they really know?

When I was chatting with Tom and detected that he thought it was really difficult, I was able to ask, "How do you know it's difficult?" It's tough to answer this question when you have never given it a go! And, of course, having never attempted it, this forced the realisation on his part that he didn't really know how difficult it was or not.

"It's a myth, it's not that difficult," I half-lied, and then I shared a few reasons why, including some diving specific information, from my experiences for performing the dive. Unlike his coach, I had multiple experiences of what it is actually like to perform it so I was able to share real experiences.

As a mentor, I always have an attitude of, "Of course you can do it; it's easy." If you describe things as difficult, people will make them difficult. Generally speaking, if you underestimate people's ability they will conform and you will get average results. If you overestimate people's ability, then extraordinary things can happen.

And in true Tom Daley-style, he attempted the dive a short time after our conversation and nailed it! The challenges he was facing with 'lost move syndrome' vanished and the perception of difficulty disappeared.

MENTOR Technique: **The reality check**

When the person you are mentoring is thinking in very definite and general terms, it's unlikely to be true so it may be very helpful to challenge the truth of their current thinking.

The most effective way of doing this is to provide a counter-example that makes them aware that the current thought-process is not true.

If a counter-example is not readily available, then gently and playfully challenge their "absolutely, completely, definitely, always, never, must, can't, have to" thought-processes.

This will be effective most of the time ***because absolute statements and thought-processes are seldom true.***

For example, if we look at sweeping generalisations, "always" is probably not always – it's more likely to be most of the time or very often, but not always.
'Everyone' is more likely to be most people, or the few people I have spoken to – it's unlikely to be everyone.

It's very efficient to think in this way – by ignoring the one time out of ten when it's not true, it allows us to think in simpler terms and remove complexity. We can be more definite in our opinions and judgements. However, we are ignoring the interesting stuff: the differences; the exceptions to the rule; and the things that are likely to provide a solution.

Being absolute and simplistic can also be a lot more polite – a little "white lie" to make our choices a little more socially acceptable. For example, if we are asked by a friend to meet for dinner when there is something else we want to do instead, we will say, "Sorry, I can't." It's not really true. We could – we are just choosing not to.

We may do this because we are already committed to the other thing, or we have already decided we really want to do something else, or the consequences of blowing out the other thing are far worse than saying no to our friend, or something like that.

Either way, it's a choice, but having made that choice, we turn it into a complete impossibility, as if it's completely outside of our ability to do anything about it – "Sorry, I can't." It's much nicer than saying, "Sorry, mate – there's something else that I would rather do."

Whatever the reasons for thinking in this way, whether to make it easier to handle complexity and have clear opinions, or to make our choices more socially acceptable by pretending that we don't have a choice, the result is we are a few cards short of playing with a full deck. We are deluding ourselves and removing options by over-simplifying the problem.

So, just to be clear, the kind of words that we say when we are making sweeping generalisations are:
Always, Never, Everyone, Nobody, Everything, Nothing, etc.

And the kind of words that we say when we are being inflexible and imposing rules or boundaries on ourselves are:

Can't, Won't, Have to, Must, Mustn't, etc.

Below are a few examples of how you can gently challenge this absolute thinking:

Simply challenge the thought process itself by doubting it:

It never happens – Really? Never? Not once?

It always happens – Really? Always? What, every time?

That won't work – Really? Not at all? Not under any circumstances? How do you know?

I can't do that – Really? It's completely impossible?

There's absolutely no way? How do you know?

Mentor

It's too difficult – Really? Too difficult to do it first time; or ever? How do you know?

Delivered with a cheeky smile, you can have some fun with this – and the result is a shift in thinking for the mentee.

One step at a time

When you are performing at the highest level, you get a lot of feedback. I could sometimes perform a dive and before doing it again, I was told: "Arms up on take-off; keep head still; look forwards; push hips up and over; extend knees, ankles and toes; squeeze into shape more; spot the water on each somersault; move arms before body on line-up; lock elbows on entry. It sounds sensible, until you consider that I have 1.5 seconds between platform and hitting the water! ***Just give me one or maybe two things to focus on.***

One of my most rewarding experiences as a mentor was spent with Justin Lee Collins. He's a presenter, comedian, celebrity and one of the nicest people that I know. He's such a genuine, humble and down-to-earth guy. We had met a few times before, when JLC was presenting a show I was involved in for E4 called 'The Games'. So we knew each other and got on well.

I had 12 days of filming in which to turn JLC into a diver; getting him as good as he could be and as high as he could go for the TV show 'JLC High Diver'. This delightful mentoring game was made even more challenging because he is extremely scared of heights. The last time he went off a diving board was when he was 11 years old.

Predictably, as we pushed open the doors to Sheffield's Ponds Forge poolside, I noticed that JLC couldn't help but glance up.

As you enter the pool area and the doors close behind, you feel a wave of humidity. It's unusual being fully clothed in a space where you would normally be in a swimsuit; it's hot and in only a few moments, beads of sweat start to appear. Your ears fill with the noise of a busy swimming pool, learn-to-swim teachers shouting their instructions, students cheering as the ball rattles in the back of the water-polo net, the lap of the water over the grates and the distant rumbling echoes of the diving boards.

Regardless of all of the sights and sounds of this busy place and despite I being the entire length of a 50m swim pool and 25m dive pool away from it, you still can't help but notice it. It's the tallest point, where all the stairs lead to, towering way above and almost looming over the shimmering water – it's the 10m board. It grabs your attention in the same way as someone does when they stand and lean over you as you sit at a table or desk. As you lift your eyes to look at the board, you feel the butterflies of nerves and excitement.

As you move along the length of the swimming pool, the top board seems to grow with each of your steps. To put it into perspective, it's the height of a double-decker bus, balanced on top of another double-decker bus, with a car on top. If you are mad enough to jump off you hit the water at nearly 40mph and you feel that impact, every time.

I could see that JLC was going through a range of primal emotions, like the feeling you get when you see the biggest roller coaster in the theme park. He stood there on the pool deck, in a tracksuit with his long hair and trademark beard. He looked terrified. As we gazed up towards the 10m diving board, he tried to make polite conversation and, in his thick Bristolian accent, said: "Now that I'm close to it, it seems so much taller." At the same time, his body language and the tone of his voice were screaming, "Oh shit, what have I got myself into here?"

On that first day, before any of the physical training started, I wanted to find out where we were, so I asked a fully clothed, nervous JLC to follow me. Off we went to the stairs, which would lead us in increments of 3m, 5m and 7.5m, up to the 10m board. It's the long walk that Justin would eventually become familiar with; when learning to dive, it's the constant climbing of the stairs that tires you out during a session!

We got halfway, I asked Justin to follow me to the edge of the 5m board. This is the height of the 'top-board' at most swimming pools and, true to form, heard the words: "Oh, my god – it seems so much higher when you're up here." These are the words I hear every time I take someone up onto the diving boards. It's true – it feels so much higher. As JLC gingerly approached the edge of the board and felt the expanse of space around him, standing away from the safety of the rails, alone, exposed, on the edge with the bottom of the pool clearly visible through the shiny water below, he said: "I can never see myself going off this 5m, Leon, it's ridiculous. I feel sick!"

We continued up the stairs all the way up to 10m. As you step out onto what feels like a helicopter landing pad, you realise that this is it. This is what all the fuss is about and quite right too – it's so high! You can see everything from here, people on the poolside look like they're miniature. You become really aware of the vast expanse of space around you, the sounds of the pool are different from this height; and it's hot, really hot. But I'm sure the height makes it feel hotter.

I looked over at Justin gripping onto the safety rail right at the back of the 10m board, with white knuckles, and the colour drained out of his face. He was shaking; I swear I could hear his heart thumping. He was frozen with fear, abject terror all over his face and holding on for dear life! We stayed up there on the 10m. I encouraged him to let go of the rail and move a little closer to the edge. At first, he was only able to do this by lying spread-eagled on the platform. Slowly he became more relaxed and we sat down in the middle of the board. I said, "Welcome to my world!" and he replied, "Leon, I'm serious. There is no way in the world I could ever go off here. It's impossible for me. I'm way too scared."

We stopped off at the 5m again on the way down and after the trauma of visiting the 10m he said, "I think I could possibly go off here, maybe." It was a marked improvement on what he felt like on the way up! Justin and I ate our lunch on the 10m platform every day during filming, gradually normalising such an alien environment.

The most effective way of tackling an impossible task is to break it down into incremental steps that are possible. Start low and slow. Let's learn how to walk before we learn how to run... let's just jump. We started from the lowest-available height, off the poolside. Once Justin had performed a jump competently from there, we would go higher to the 1m board, then up to the 3m, and once confidence and competency had been achieved, up we went again, this time to the 5m and so on.

During this time, my attention was on building rapport, trust and confidence by moving Justin along swiftly and safely. After each attempt, I would let him know how well he was doing, what he was doing correctly (in order that he kept doing that) and also what to do differently on his next attempt. As we progressed, I could see his surprise and delight in what he was accomplishing mixed with some trepidation about the next step! Every time I noticed the fear creep back in; this usually happened whenever we went up a level of diving board, I would remind him that he had already overcome this feeling and it was just excitement about the next achievement.

This strategy was successful, and eventually Justin was able to start diving in head-first and moving up the heights of diving boards. There was no need to turn it into a debate or conversation. I would simply move up to the next board without saying anything and JLC would know he was ready; time to progress. My actions spoke louder than words, he had complete trust and confidence in me, so that when I encouraged him to progress higher or to a more difficult dive – and even though his head was screaming 'no' – he went with me. I would almost rush him in order to prevent his conscious mind from getting involved and keep his attention on the process. I would do this by swiftly moving him to the end of the board and before he had time to talk himself out of it I would count "3,2,1... GO!"

During the filming, he jumped from the 10m board where only weeks earlier a white-faced JLC couldn't even get within two metres of the edge. He even dived from the 7.5m, a truly incredible achievement. Not bad for someone who said on our first day together that he could never go off a 5m board and that going off a 10m platform was just too ridiculous to even consider!

A few days away from the completion of the filming, where JLC was due to perform in front of an international audience, disaster struck. He was practising one of his dives from the 5m board and as he hit the water he somehow perforated his eardrum. The ear specialist said JLC needed six weeks out of the water. He was gutted and filming was delayed until he was given the all-clear.

The production company's idea was to set up a dramatic climax to the show. JLC would compete against veteran divers, at his local pool in Bristol where he once took his first-ever dive as a young boy. The competition would be in front of a packed audience including his dad, wife and two children. It was six weeks since the accident and we had four hours before the competition was due to start to get him ready. He was terrified, not only of competing but also of hurting his ear once again. All the confidence he had built up with me had vanished, and he was back to where we started. We had a mountain to climb, once again, this time much quicker and with the cameras rolling every step of the way.

So my job as his mentor was to instil as much confidence as quickly as possible. I knew that making assertions (you must do it) would result only in resistance. Instead, I provided him with a choice, which wasn't really a choice at all. I said: 'It's totally up to you; **you can do it** if you want to; **you will be ok**; but it's up to you. Off you go!' All the bits in bold were accompanied by the Leon Nod.

JLC was just brilliant – not only did he get back on the horse; he did it with some style. He overcame the fears of his ear and of the technical dives and performed in front of a packed audience. He came third in the competition. I will never forget the moment after it was all done. I looked over and saw the beaming smile on his face. This is what it's all about for me as his proud mentor; the joy of seeing him succeed and most importantly enjoying it so much.

MENTOR Techniques For 'live' coaching/ mentoring

In sport, you have the advantage of working in the performance context rather than just talking about it, eg, I'm standing next to JLC on the board right before he dives and able to give instant feedback as soon as he has performed.

I'm aware that in other activities it's less easy to have someone on you shoulder providing feedback in real time, but if you have the opportunity to work in the real performance context, I suggest that you take every opportunity to do so. It's so much more effective than talking about it before/after the event.

If you, as the coach or mentor, are there at the time, you can set objectives and make adjustments in response to what is happening in the moment.

I would recommend the following approaches:

Getting Started

Begin with a huge objective/goal that is motivational to the person you are working with, and then break it down into incremental stages. Find out where you are starting from, and then take the next step.

During the process of moving towards the goal, there is no point working with anything other than the individual's

current performance. If you were in London at Trafalgar Square and someone asked you for guidance to get to St Paul's Cathedral you will not help them by describing what St. Paul's looks like: "Big white building, dome on top – they cleaned it a couple of years ago; looks great."
You need to start from where they are in the now and provide adjustments or extra instructions to move them in the direction towards their objective/goal.

Making tasks scalable

As you add instructions, tasks or adjustments it's important that they are difficult enough to stretch the individual, but not completely out of their reach.
If a task is too easy, it's not engaging – the individual will not need to get into a higher performance state to achieve it and will not get a rush from achieving it. Some coaches/trainers/ mentors who are controlling actually slow down the people that they are attempting to help. It's best if the pace is set by the person you are working with!

On the other hand, setting tasks that are completely out of reach can have negative effects. It can dent confidence, or the individual may disengage.

Bumping up against a boundary

Occasionally you will find that individuals set a firm boundary between comfortable and uncomfortable, or what they can and can't achieve; a specific point at which the person decides, "I can do that, but not that."

When you explore the boundary, it's not fixed – because it doesn't exist other than in that person's thoughts.

The game here is to get people to make evaluations from experience, not from the prejudices. I'm always amused when people say "I can't do that" and when I ask if they tried, they say no. How can you possibly know what you can and can't do if you have never had a crack at it?

Let me use a simple example to illustrate. Imagine that you are working with someone who is afraid of heights and will not climb a ladder. When you ask at what point does it become too high they will probably provide an answer like, "The 5th rung." Start with where they are comfortable, will both feet on the first rung. From there, rising one foot to the second rung is not such a big deal; it's easy. If they can do that, they can probably move their bottom foot to the 3rd rung and feel comfortable, and so on until you reach the boundary. Let's imagine the threshold is the 5th rung and they have moved to the 4th: Confirm that the 4th rung is comfortable and then begin to observe what a tiny difference there is between the 4th and 5th. Invite them to step up to the 5th only for a second, and get them to step back down before they have had a chance to do so themselves, at the same time affirming how easy it was.

Then ask them to do it again for a few seconds. Repeat this fractionated process until they feel comfortable on the 5th and ask them to notice what a small difference there is between the 5th and 6th.

If you can get them to the 6th or 7th, invite them back down to look at the ladder again and tell you where the boundary is now... It will be difficult for them to insist that it has not changed, and the reality of the boundary begins to crumble. Once the boundaries are less hard and fast, it becomes easier to question or challenge them.

Again, scalability is important, you need to be creating a little bit of discomfort so that, with time, reassurance and a bit of conscious breathing, it becomes comfortable.

If you create a huge discomfort, the individual may panic and it's difficult (but not impossible) to get them back once they have entered a highly emotive and irrational state.

Bumping against a limiting belief

I could have told Justin a story that would have helped him a bit, but nothing could have been as effective as eating our lunch while sitting on top of the 10m diving board.

Whatever someone thinks they can't do, take them somewhere and create an experience that shows them they can – there is no bigger persuader and no better way to re-wire someone's thinking than a real experience.

So, just as with boundaries, the intention when working with self-imposed limitations is to make them untrue by providing an irrefutable counter-experience.

Beliefs can be quite sticky because, as a thought process, they are very closed-minded so you may need to trick people a bit in order to get them to play. Once we really believe something, we will notice evidence that supports it, ignore the evidence that contradicts it and go to extraordinary lengths to avoid any experience that could make the belief untrue. Sometimes it's worth staging the context a bit (eg. A helpful stooge in the audience) to make sure that the counter-experience is safe or positive.

Keeping it up! Owning and sustaining changes

With many mentoring, coaching, or training initiatives, people ask, "How do we make people engage?" Or "how do we sustain it?" The answer is you don't – they do.

This attitude of mentors/coaches/trainers taking responsibility for other people's development is not the solution to the problem of engagement and ongoing development – it's the cause of the problem.

Mentor

We live in a culture of instant gratification and "fix me now". There's no better example than where an athlete goes to see the physiotherapist with an injury and says, "I'm broken – please fix me". The physio treats the athlete and then sets a series of exercises to be done each day before the next session. The athlete comes back a week later still with the injury. The physio asks, "How have you been getting on with those exercises?" and the answer is, "Oh, I forgot/couldn't be bothered/didn't have time/etc." The athlete has not taken personal responsibility for fixing the problem and is trying to make it the physio's problem.

You can't change people – you can create experiences that provoke them to change themselves. You can't teach people – you can create experiences that motivate them to learn. You can't fix people – you can help them to fix themselves.

With mentoring, or any development experience, I would suggest that you make sure that the mentee does not park the responsibility for their performance at your front door.

One way to ensure that the mentee owns the process is tasking. If the entire mentoring relationship is limited to the time you are together it can become reflective and way too passive on the part of the mentee. There is a need to provide real-world challenges and tasks for your mentee.

One step at a time

I tend to set myself tasks or stretches to keep me stimulated, alive and learning. I often have fun with my friends by agreeing to somehow get irrelevant words into my presentations/ commentary. It's a lot of fun but, at the same time, takes some of the nerves away and gets me into a higher performance state. I love anything that prevents me from creating a comfort zone and simply going through the motions.

The 'art' of mentoring – storytelling and creating experiences

Whenever you think of "wisdom", the archetypal character that appears in your mind is probably a calm, silver-haired person who gazes wistfully into the distance and then slowly and calmly 'spins a yarn' of a story that carries profound meaning. If ever you have had the good fortune to be around elders who behave in this way, you will be aware how hypnotically engaging these stories can be to a young and curious mind.

The direct way that we now communicate via all kinds of media is a fairly recent development. For centuries, we as humans have evolved through telling stories and sharing experiences. We find it easy to take deep and complex meaning from stories and experiences; it's memorable and it's how we learn best.

When we communicate specifically and directly it is seldom remembered long-term and only provides knowledge; it does not provoke deep understanding or change in behaviour. Besides, as I mentioned earlier, if the person you are mentoring is stressed or inflexible direct communication 'bounces off' and every suggestion will be met with a counter-challenge – "I've thought of that, I can't do that, I've already done that, etc."

> ***"Advice is like snow; the softer it falls, the longer it dwells upon, and the deeper it sinks into the mind"***
> ***Samuel Taylor Coleridge***

Great stories that are descriptive enough to be engaging take the person away from the here-and-now, and completely bypass resistance. It's impossible to deflect if the communication is indirect.

It's extremely helpful for getting past the professional shell, or in the case of world-class athletes, their media-trained answers.

This book is hopefully an example of this story-telling process. If it only featured the mentoring techniques, it would not be much fun to read and there would not be as much depth of meaning without the stories to bring it to life.

By way of example, I'd like to throw in a couple more stories for good measure.

I'd heard a lot about Dr Steve Peters. He was a former forensic psychiatrist, the guy who used to work for the government assessing whether psychopaths/sociopaths were fit to rejoin society or not. It sounds like an interesting job! He had recently decided to challenge himself further and he was now working with elite athletes; he often jests it was much safer in his previous job!

Steve was presenting in October 2007, near Sheffield, which was my training base, so it made a lot of sense to head along. He was, after all, the name on everyone's lips, working with many of GB's top athletes in the build-up to the 2008 Olympic Games, including the GB cycling team. I couldn't wait to hear what this guy had to say.

The conference, called Mind Games, was being delivered at a beautiful country hall just outside Sheffield. Steve was the only presenter, and there were about 60 other keen attendees, from all over the UK, from a mixture of backgrounds and sports, a real eclectic mix. The room was buzzing with excitement, coffee cups being clinked as people realised it was time to take their seats. The anticipation was building: what's it going to be like? Who is this guy? How come everyone is raving about him? What is in store for us and what are we going to learn?

Steve Peters stood up and strolled to the centre of the stage with a self-assured air and the crowd fell into silence, and even the people who weren't facing forward quickly found their space. It was as if we were all under a spell, and we stared towards him. Steve is of average height, has light coloured hair and was wearing trousers and a shirt. Nothing about his appearance gave cause for undivided attention, but as soon as he stood up, he had it. And then we were off, straight into it. He began by setting the scene: what we were there for, to find out how the mind works and how we can get a rise in performance as a result of knowing this. Sign me up, please. I was training towards the 2008 Olympic Games, which would have been my fourth, I'm a sponge when it comes to this stuff – "tell me more; you have my full attention". I think it's important to never stop learning.

Within moments Steve was sharing his rules of life: there were three of them and they apply to everyone, in any situation, whoever you are in the world and whatever you do in life. He then flicked to the next slide to show three hard-hitting, succinct bullet-points.

Life is not fair

The goalposts always move

Your job is to do your best under the circumstances

The whole room murmured and nodded – how did he do that? In three bullet points, Dr Steve Peters had scooped up what each of us had experienced throughout our lives so many times and had boiled it down to these three rules. It made such sense to everyone in the audience. Since that day, I always quote Steve and his three rules of life when I'm presenting.

At the time of writing this book, I don't have any children of my own, I do have many friends who have, and I love to watch their kids play.

I would watch from afar as watch from afar as Pete Waterfield's son Lewis would dive around on the floor, then up on and off the sofa whilst holding his latest action figures, constructing an imaginary battlefield, taking on the roles of each of the characters in turn by changing the sound of his voice and facial expression from frowns to wide-eyed surprise. I had no idea who was who, what was going on and it didn't matter a bit, I was mesmerised. He was five years old and was playing on his own and had been for well over an hour. Completely engaged, lost in his own little world, Lewis was having an absolute ball.

At no point when I was watching and pretending to work on my laptop did he stop what he was doing, look over at me and ask, "Am I doing this right? Is this the correct way to play with my action figures?"

And I began to wonder, how, as adults, we develop a concern about what other people may think of our activities. We want to be seen to be good or do things well – and we do what we can to avoid people thinking we are wrong. We tend to forget that we are all still a work-in-progress and fall under a spell of thinking that we are a finished product. We attempt to avoid errors – but there is trial and error involved in every learning process – if we are scared of making mistakes we will never grow. This is how, as children, we learned almost everything. Imagine if we took the "too scared to make mistakes approach" when we were learning to walk. After a few attempts to walk and after falling over a few times, we declare: "Walking is not for me. I've tried it a few times now, and it's too difficult. I'm going to stick to crawling!"

"We don't stop playing because we grow old – we grow old because we stop playing"
George Bernard Shaw

Mentor

"The bloke who never made any mistakes, never actually did anything" Lord Alan Sugar

To perform at the highest level, it helps to ignore the subjective judgements of others and pay attention only to your performance. Focus only on the process - not on the outcome. The outcome is often out of your control but the process is very much within your control.

As I stood on the edge of the platform in Athens about to dive, I could feel Pete standing a few feet away and breathing in sync, the 18000 strong crowd fell silent and in that moment we needed to perform. After my long four-year road to recovery, despite all of the interruptions to my training, in that moment I felt better equipped than I had been at the previous Olympics where we came in fourth.

I was better equipped mentally. In Sydney I had gone there to win an Olympic medal, which was all I focused on. In Athens I went there to put in an Olympic medal-winning performance and ignored the scoreboard throughout the competition. I focused on what I had within my control and ignored everything outside of my control, allowing me to perform at my best when it mattered the most. "Control the controllable" - you can't win an Olympic medal but you can put in a medal-winning performance.

MENTOR technique: **Making your stories metaphoric, colourful and engaging**

You can use the following process to come up with colourful stories that really hit the mark:

1. Listen

2. Ask yourself, "What is the thought-process they are running that is limiting them?" Is it an unhelpful belief about someone or something? For example, have they got their crystal ball out and made predictions about what will happen or what people will do in the future? Are they being: judgmental, finger-wagging, taking their toys home, blowing it out of proportion, obsessing about one detail, doing the same thing over and over again and expecting a different result? Or just that they can't do it?

3. The next step is to work out what the solution is to that thought-process – what would contradict it? What would make it untrue? What are they ignoring in order to think this way? What are they pretending to themselves?

4. Once you have an idea of how their thinking needs to change to free them from the ditch, ask yourself, "What's it a bit like?"

then grab an example of the solution in another context and tell a story about it. You may have an example from your hobby or interest, from the world of sport, from a biography you read once, from something your grandmother used to say. See what bubbles up. When telling the story, to make it extremely effective, you need to be as descriptive as you can – don't just talk about it, but paint a picture of how the experience felt with your words. Use sights, sounds and feelings. Bring it to life and make it as real as possible – rather than factually reporting on it.

5. When telling the story and sharing a solution within the story, make sure you do not 'spell it out' to the mentee, by linking the story back to their 'issue' otherwise the metaphor loses its power and becomes advice. It works much more effectively if you allow the metaphor to sink in and for their unconscious mind to make sense of it. Like the lyrics to a song, everyone will have a different interpretation of the exact meaning of a story, but the metaphor works at the deeper level.

6. It's ok to have a go, and it's fine for it not to work. You can't do any harm just by telling a story, although you may feel a little odd at first when answering a question with what may seem to be an unrelated story. Trust me; after a few goes you'll love it. Especially when you 'hit the jackpot'; the mentee's issue vanishes and they are left there with no idea what you've done or what the issue was in the first place. You'll know when it's worked because you will see it in their face. That's the joy of being a great mentor and using this approach – it's a Jedi skill!

How far can you go with it?

By now, you can probably tell that I'm passionate about this mentoring stuff. I tend to refer to it as a forgotten art in our society, and I think the benefits, if done well, are extraordinary. In my opinion it's the best way to engage and nurture talent in any field.

When people learn any complex skill, craft, trade or technical ability there is usually a lot of shadowing or apprenticeship involved. This is how it's always been; we have passed on our entire culture through mentoring.

Being mentored is an essential part of growth and being a mentor is an essential and deeply rewarding part of maturity.

> ***"The unselfish effort to bring cheer to others will be the beginning of a happier life for ourselves"***
> ***Helen Keller***

I recently had the pleasure of meeting a really interesting guy called Tim Kiy. He's very senior in one of the Big Four high-street banks. We shared the stage at an event on 'mentoring' and Tim said a few things that were really interesting from a corporate perspective. As well as the flattering feedback that comes from being asked to be someone's mentor (and it's really interesting to get value from that feedback by asking why they chose you) there are practical business advantages to being a mentor. Tim describes how, through mentoring he is able to gain a deep understanding of what's really going on within the business, in a way that no report or summary would have allowed.

I would like to give you an idea of why I care so much.

How far can you go with it?

I certainly wouldn't be where I am today without the help, support and guidance of others. It would be remiss of me not to mention my amazing parents, Sue and Roy. Without their creativity in dealing with me as a youngster, this would have been a very different story.

To say I was a challenging child would be an understatement, I listen to the stories and think of my poor parents and what they had to deal with. I also think what superb solutions they came up with under the circumstances.

I was born in a pike position – much to the doctors' surprise and my mum's horror I was a breach birth and was born bottom-first. Not the nicest start but there was so much more to come. I am my parents' first child and so they had nothing to compare me to other than their friends' experiences. These were very different to what they were going through. I would cry and scream, I'm sure most babies do, but I would really cry and scream; loud, blood-curdling screams relentlessly night after night. My parents were told: "You just need to leave him, then he will eventually cry himself to sleep." But I never did.

Mrs. Mann was the healthcare worker assigned to my mum and dad; she was by no means new to healthcare and as her name seemed to suggest, she was tough, super-tough. After my mum and dad had struggled in vain to deal with me, I just would not settle when they put me down to sleep, Mrs. Mann came round to show them how it was done. She probably just thought that my mum and dad, first-time parents, were struggling with parenthood. Dealing with crying babies who won't settle was what she does best – or did, I even broke supernanny! Even Mrs. Mann couldn't leave me to fall asleep when I was crying; that must have been quite something.

Of course it didn't stop there, as I grew from baby to toddler the challenges for my parents kept on coming. I was so demanding and had so much energy that my parents decided to take me to the family doctor to see if there was anything wrong with me. The doctor said there was nothing medically wrong with me, there weren't as many labels back then ADD, ADHD, etc. I was just labelled as a problem child (by the doctors, not my parents, although they might have agreed strongly). My parents were given two choices. "Would you like us to take Leon off you and we can sedate him?" or "would you like to try to deal with him?"

My parents choose the latter, although now they needed a new strategy. Maybe they could give me to other people, so they could look after me for a bit and my parents could get a break – unfortunately they lost friends and ran out of willing victims. So they decided to fight fire with fire and said, "let's try to tire the little b*****d out" and so my life of intense activity began. I was taken on long walks, constantly being engaged with, bounced in my babywalker and anything else my parents could come up with to grab my attention and wear me out! I started swimming while in nappies and started 'tumble tots' (mother and baby gymnastics) as soon as I was old enough. Interestingly, the reason my mum chose 'tumble tots' wasn't because she had any interest in gymnastics but because I was so uncoordinated (and still am to this day). My parents used to joke that I could fall over sitting down! So I was always black and blue.

The nature vs nurture debate is an interesting one and if any of you ever see me try something requiring coordination, I'm certainly not what you may describe as a 'natural' – however, I will be there long after everyone else has gone home, continuing to practise.

My early years were a string of hyperactive near-disasters. At 18 months, I escaped from the house and climbed a ladder on to the roof. My dad rescued me moments before I started my diving career early. After a close-run contest with a stair gate, I lost and fell the height of the stairs, bouncing off the wall at the bottom and nearly landing on the dining-room table.

How far can you go with it?

As I got older the difficulties continued; I tried judo and became the only person to be thrown out of a martial arts class for fighting! Once again my parents were told: "Please don't bring Leon back, he's too disruptive."

One day I even asked my parents if I could change my name.

Me: "I don't like my name."

Dad: "Why don't you like your name, Leon?"

Me: "Because Leon is always in trouble."

School was a huge challenge for me. My overexuberance meant that other children I played with would get hurt, and my attention span made the structured classroom feel like torture. I just wanted to do physical stuff. My parents used this as a motivation: if any of my teachers said I wasn't concentrating or putting in maximum effort, they would reduce my swimming/gym/diving privileges. *Thanks, mum and dad.*

As a child, my default answer to the question, "Do you want to try [insert name of sport/activity]?" was 'yes!' – I tried everything and if I didn't enjoy it after a few goes, I would move on to try something new. After a couple of comical, uncoordinated attempts and much to my dad's disappointment it was clear that I wasn't going to be a footballer. When I stared diving at eight, it was just one of many sports I tried during my active childhood, but this one was different because I quickly became quite good. Diving became my favourite sport and the rest, as you say, is history.

Looking back on my life, I feel privileged to have been supported and challenged by so many different mentors. I learnt many different things from each relationship and the more I reflect, the more I realise how important the role of a mentor is in a journey

Our opportunity to achieve is strongly influenced by how supportive and creative our guardians and mentors are. If you are a mentor, your support and creativity will influence fundamental changes that will serve the person that you are mentoring for the rest of their life – ***few relationships are so deeply rewarding.***

Sadly, the mentoring relationship comes to an end, as it should.

When I met Tom he was 10 and I was his hero. He's now a young man, World Champion, Commonwealth Champion, good-looking, articulate, intelligent, he got nine GCSEs, mostly A*, and he even got Kate Moss to pose for his GCSE photography project. We are nearing the end of our journey as mentor and mentee, and he's now my hero!

It's important to recognise that, as a mentor, you are helping with a period of growth, hopefully without them becoming dependent upon your guidance indefinitely. The objective is that mentee spreads their wings and becomes independent.

Having achieved at the highest level within my chosen field, I'm left with a deep feeling of gratitude toward all of the names on the back of my Olympic medal, my mentors. It now fills me with such excitement and pride to know that my name, among many others will be on the back of future medals – whether it is a medal, or something else that represents their achievement. And I'm so passionate about this subject of mentoring, because I believe it's the way forward in nurturing future talent.

Thanks for reading my book. If you are on your way up, I hope that you are able to attract creative and flexible mentors, and if you are already there I hope that you experience the joy of giving something of yourself to someone else through a mentoring relationship.